- **Meditate**

The goal of meditation is to quiet the mind. Mindfulness is the practice of bringing one's attention to the here and now, with the intention of being more attuned to one's internal and external environments.

Everyday living requires constant mental processing. We never stop considering our to-do lists, our dinner plans, our past actions, and the alternatives we might have taken. Even though meditation

may seem obvious, but consider isn't
about silencing your mind, it's a
great opportunity to take a break
from the bustle of daily life and
focus within, where you may more
objectively observe your thoughts
and feelings without judgment.

MEDITATIVE NOTES

- **Disconnect from your social media accounts for a while.**

This how much time most of us spend staring at devices. Social media may be the single most important factor disturbing people's serenity. When we compare our own lives on social media to the lives of our friends and celebrities, it's easy to feel like we're falling short. This will be enough to shake up your equilibrium.

Furthermore, studies have shown that prolonged social media use is associated with negative physiological changes in the brain. Since our bodies release dopamine (the joyful hormone) every time we post or get a signal from an app, this reduces our capacity to maintain our attention on any one specified issue and makes us addicted to our screens. Brain scans of chronic social media users resemble those of drug and gambling addicts, according to research.

If you value your mental health, it's wise to minimize your phone use as much as possible.

MEDITATIVE NOTES

- **To train one's breathing**

Consider your breathing to be the universal remote for your ANS. In just a few seconds, you may alter your mood just by adjusting your breathing pattern.

Do you need to relax or calm down? Inducing the relaxation response in the body through controlled, steady breathing reduces blood pressure, calms the nervous system, and eases the mind. Just sit there for a moment, shut your eyes, and focus on deep belly breathing. A sense of peace will begin to permeate your being shortly.

One of the simplest and most direct routes to calming oneself down is to focus on one's breathing.

MEDITATIVE NOTES

- **Treat others (and yourself) with compassion.**

It's impossible to be down when you're actively helping folks around you. Focusing on the positive will attract more positive experiences, and you'll feel more at ease as your mind shifts its attention away from what's bothering you.

Practicing everyday acts of kindness can be a great stress reliever. As you help others, don't lose sight of your own needs. If you're gentle with yourself, you'll likely be gentle with others. Engage in pursuits that bring you joy and uplift your spirit. The path to a happier, more fulfilled life is paved with love, both for oneself and for others.

MEDITATIVE NOTES

- **Get outside and enjoy nature.**

The splendor of nature is beyond compare. The simple act of being in nature has been shown to have a positive effect on mood and health. Positive mental health and the avoidance of suffering are strongly correlated with the degree to which one engages with nature in the forms of observation, reflection, and appreciation.

Those who spend more time outside tend to be more fulfilled by their lives and report higher levels of happiness, according to scientific studies. Daily walks in natural settings, such as the woods or by the river, are excellent for relieving tension and anxiety, but even a stroll around the park right outside your front door can have a positive effect.

Spending time in nature is a tried-and-true method for calming the mind and heart.

MEDITATIVE NOTES

- **Have as much fun as possible**

Laughter is the finest medication since it alleviates almost all symptoms. Laughter increases resistance to disease, decreases stress hormones, lessens discomfort, relaxes muscles, prevents heart disease, brightens your outlook on life, calms your nerves, lightens your load, lifts your spirits, fortifies your resolve, forges bonds within a group, and soothes the tensions that threaten to derail positive interactions.

You can't find calm within yourself if you treat life too seriously. The invitation is to keep looking for the good and beautiful in a life that can be difficult, stressful, and full of surprises.

If you're struggling and your mind is testing you, seek out the things that make you happy. Whatever makes you happy—a humorous movie, a night out with friends, or just a little dancing in the living room—do that.

MEDITATIVE NOTES

- **Speak your mind**

Finding and maintaining your own inner calm is essential to your creative process. The act of creative expression, in any form, is beneficial to one's health. It's a great way to practice mindfulness because it forces you to zero in on the task at hand, concentrate intently on every aspect of it, and enter a state of flow in which you forget the passage of time altogether.

Whether it's producing music, sketching a picture, or painting a chair, engaging in creative activity calms the mind and diverts attention from negative thoughts and feelings.

Do you feel like you have no imagination? You're wrong. Everyone has a creative side just by being alive. Also, you don't have to reach Picasso status in order to create art. Stop worrying about failure and just do it.

MEDITATIVE NOTES

- **Maintain a constant state of awareness**

Practicing mindfulness can help you live in the moment and alleviate stress. Meditation can help you do this by encouraging you to look inward. Mindfulness is not something that requires you to sit quietly with your eyes closed. Why not give your best effort to remain awake and mindful throughout the day?

You may easily bring your focus back to the here and now at any point throughout the day. A tranquil mind is one that is present in the moment and not preoccupied with the past or the future. How can you help? At the first sign of an intrusive thought or emotion, redirect your focus to something more immediate, such as your breathing, the feelings in your body, or a simple activity like sipping your coffee.

Give it your full focus and try to bring your thoughts into harmony with the here and now as much as possible. True calm only exists in the present moment.

MEDITATIVE NOTES

- **Believe Every Word**

As 2 Corinthians 1:20 (NKJV) puts it, "For all the promises of God in Him are Yes, and in Him are Amen, to the glory of God through us."

Regaining your serenity will require returning to the very spot from whence it was taken - God's promises. There is nothing to worry about, nothing to question, and nothing to think about if you truly believe, if you know, that God's promises are "yes" and "amen" for you. To steal your tranquility, the devil must attack where it hurts the most: your trust in THE BLESSING.

He sees that you already have everything God has promised you. His only chance of getting them back is to convince you that he's telling the truth. You can say, "I want the promises of God, and I believe in them." And yet, do you really think they'll show up? How certain are you that you will achieve your goals, or do you ever question that you will? Satan waits to attack your faith at the precise point where your belief and disbelief meet.

Let's correct the record. God's every promise is yours. Trusting God fully is the surest way to tranquility. Jesus bore the rebuke for our peace so that we could experience the sort of peace that beyond understanding every day, in every facet of our lives.

MEDITATIVE NOTES

- **Do not give in to the Triple Threat**

My parting gift to you is tranquility of spirit. My gift of tranquility is something the world cannot provide. Don't worry or be frightened. -John 14:27

Have you ever thought how nice it would be to have some peace of mind? What is its origin? Abundance, joy, blessings, and serenity are the results of one of three potent Spirit-given gifts. Just what are they? Love, hope, and faith. Together, they can't be stopped, stopped, or contained. They are powerful enough to stop the devil himself in his tracks. They're like a three-headed monster, a triple threat to the opposition.

Satan, on the other hand, is a fraud and an antagonist. So, in an effort to undo your triumph and take your tranquility, he has devised his own triple threat. Together, they accomplish the exact opposite of what was intended (war). The worst part is that these behaviors are not just acceptable in our society but actively encouraged. You might even come to accept them as routine. What are Satan's threefold dangers? Fear, worry, and uncertainty.

God never meant for us to have to deal with uncertainties, anxieties, or fears. In addition to the mental anguish they cause, they also have a real, tangible impact on our bodies. In fact, research shows that stress can negatively impact your health, productivity, and quality of sleep. You can't change God's mind!

You have to realize that the presence of God is what brings about true peace, not the absence of problems. This means that you can rest in God's peace regardless of your current situation, no matter how dire it may seem. When you can achieve that level of calm, the rest of your life falls into place.

MEDITATIVE NOTES

- **Trust Your Conscience**

To think with the flesh is to die, but to think spiritually is to have eternal life and perfect tranquility. Romans 8:16 (NKJV) says, "The Spirit Himself testifies with our spirit, that we are children of God."

It's true that the devil and other people can disrupt our serenity on occasion, but most of the time, we have only ourselves to blame. Christians might lose the joy and contentment we were created for when we make wrong decisions and ignore God's voice.

What can we do to prevent this?

Intuitively, by tuning in to one's own advice. At some point in your life, you may have been in a sticky situation when you needed direction but weren't sure what to do, despite praying and reading the Bible. Perhaps there was a question that the Bible didn't answer directly, such as which city to settle in.

MEDITATIVE NOTES

- **Respect Other People**

To paraphrase 1 Corinthians 13:8 (NKJV): "Love never fails."

Love is eternal. That's like the secret to winning every time. The two most important rules in the Bible are love for God and love for others. Sounds easy, yet many of us have trouble doing it in practice.

How come maintaining an attitude of love is vital? If you don't, someone will disturb your tranquility. Satan will take note of your progress in faith if you have been spending significant time in God's Word, relying on His promises, and professing His truth over your life. He intends to steal, kill, and destroy (what you have), so beware. How? He will employ both chance and human interaction.

People, he knows, have a way of seriously disrupting our day, our calm, and our happiness. If he thinks he can throw you off track by sending someone to ruffle your feathers, he will. Your mission is to avoid falling for the trap.

Violence undermines social harmony. An unforgiving heart is poison to happiness. What's the remedy? Dating by walking.

As Jesus said in John 13:34 (NIRV), "Love one another, just as I have loved you." One that has mercy for the worst of sinners and grace for those who don't deserve it.

MEDITATIVE NOTES

Made in the USA
Columbia, SC
09 October 2024